MW01596025

POEMS FROM EARTH AND WIND

POEMS FROM EARTH AND WIND

BY

SHEILA HANDLER

Copyright © 2007 by Sheila Handler. All rights reserved. No part of this book may be reproduced, transmitted, or utilized in any form by any means without the written permission from the author, except for the inclusion of brief quotations in a review.

PUBLISHED BY
Sheila Handler
P.O. Box 1846
Provincetown, Massachusetts 02657

Library of Congress Control Number: 2007902819
ISBN: 978-0-9710018-3-1
Printed in the United States of America
First Edition

Cover by Carlos Murguía Aguilar, Provincetown
Edited by Lester Handler

ABOUT THE AUTHOR

Sheila Handler was born on May 23, 1940 in Jersey City, New Jersey. A retired high school teacher of Advanced Placement Spanish Literature, the author was also a bilingual puppeteer and artist-in-residence for the New Jersey State Council on the Arts. She has dedicated her lifelong career to the well being of children, an interest expressed through teaching, puppetry and poetry.

POEMS FROM EARTH AND WIND is the author's fourth collection of lyric poetry. In it she continues to utilize flashback, social issues and the beauty of both nature and travel for inspiration. The author has published three previous works: POEMS OF A HAUNTED CHILD, A POET'S JOURNEY TOWARD SEPTEMBER 11 and FALLING INTO THE SKY.

Ms. Handler's poetry collections become a spiritual journey in which she contemplates the passage of time, the healing beauty of nature, the joys of being a grandmother and the commonality of human experience and anguish. She shares her retirement with her husband, Les, and takes great delight in her children and grandchildren.

DEDICATION

This collection of poems is dedicated to Les, my husband of forty six years, without whose love my journey would not have been possible.

It is dedicated as well to my children and grandchildren, the inspiration of many cherished images.

<u>CONTENTS</u>

SITTING HERE

Sitting here in this
quiet moment, so
exceptional in the
journey that is my
life or redundant
path, circumventing
more truth than I would
like to admit to,
I need to embrace
the music emerging

from the air that
surrounds me softly with
the sound of love revealed,
the sonata sung
by the voices of
those I may have known,
until the crescendo
reaches my open heart,
touches my soaring soul,
lifts me from my very chair.

TO LIVE SIMPLY

To live simply
with my feet
touching earth
is to walk
alongside God.

To breathe deeply
with my breath
joining sky
is to share
Heaven's air.

To think purely
with my mind
filled with love
is to live
the poet's life.

A LOVE SONG –To Steve and Denise

When the wind calls our name
we will send our own voices
soaring, our fugal song
weaving its complex melody
into a symphony of the soul.

When the sands of time gather
collecting about our ageing feet,
we will not walk quickly
but gather our memories of love
with a slow and measured pace.

Two lovers emit a single light
that cannot be extinguished,
kindness and passion entwined
forever in our secret heart.

SONGS OF THE SEA

I. INFINITE BLUE

Infinite blue above me,
beneath me, surrounding
the boat with waves of
azure or turquoise, jade green
swirls with white lace edges
trimming the sea canvas
with silvery silence.

Infinite blue above me,
beneath me, visiting
my open soul with visions of
mystical dolphins whispering
their almost silent song,
heard only in seaborne dreams
that visit my nautical sleep.

Infinite blue above me,
beneath me, connecting
my heart to the ever pulsing
rhythm that carries my
sharpened senses now closer
to the heart of the universe,
to the soul of the open sea.

II. AT SEA

The lucky horseshoe horizon
curves placidly under the
sea dome sky, painted
with impressionistic white
strokes that decorate the
light blue canvas hung behind.

The Rotterdam sails gently,
its azure wake parting the
navy blue ocean, barely ruffled
as it stretches toward the infinite,
breezes curling the pages of
my empty notebook as I write.

My heart opens to the deep blue
palette encircling me, pulsing
its rhythmic embrace of the sea,
fathoms of light and shadow
above and beneath reflecting
memories of disappearing shore.

III. SEA SONNET

I greet the sea with my
morning smile, open to
limitless fantasies that
fly toward the mute horizon.

My heart leaps over gently
formed waves, fathoms of entwined
shadows joined beneath the
surface of the wide ocean,

the hush of sighing water
stroking the starboard side of
the ship with its cradle song

lullaby of gathering currents,
a rhythmic embrace that holds
me close to the heart of the sea.

IV. THE SEA CALLS MY NAME

The sea calls my name,
repeating the sound with
each newborn wave under
a perfect backdrop sky.

My heart must respond
to the rhythmic chant
it has endlessly heard
for eons uncounted,

its passacaglia pulsing
with a secret yearning.
I long for the dolphin's
life and journey, his cries

careening through sacred
waters before time was
even named, before the
seagull came to know the sea.

HANDS AROUND THE WORLD

Following the sun you
can almost see the path
to heaven from Herring
Cove Beach, especially
at sunset under a
translucent whitewashed sky,
the setting sun semi
hiding in a twilight mist,
but inviting me to
watch it slide toward some
unfolding West. There,
children hold hands tightly
inside a rose colored channel
as it opens to others even
further away, seeking the
westernmost seas we can know,
their hands encircling the globe,
their open hearts indicating
the ancient path of love to
heaven, eyes upon the setting sun.

STORM COMING

Storm coming,
offering
possibilities
of wind blown
destinies
not conceived
before yesterday,
but unknown
before tomorrow.

A LIFE LAST SEEN

A life last seen hiding
deep in ocean cages,
walls of water high
and infinitely wide,
so artfully blue
under porcelain skies
I never painted.
My last glimpse was so brief,
a molecular minute,
but memory is my servant
and won't let me forget
the life last seen hiding.

AFTER THE HURRICANE

I hear your voice calling,
pleading with the silent
powers of the universe,
asking to be rescued from
implacable flood water
rising over your world,
now hidden in an ocean
of tears as memories
float by, lost
in uncountable ways.

I hear your voice calling
although you can't hear mine
although my prayers are mute
although my feet now walk
on ground I know so well
but yes, there is no doubt
I hear your voice calling
across the floating graves,
above the buried screams,
into my sad but helpless ears.

SYMPHONY

The winds carry
errant messages
of a grieving
and joyous world
that I can hear
only with my soul,
open to the words
and healing music
that surround me in
a cocoon of whispers.

If only I knew
exactly how
I could record
this sweet symphony,
I would copy the notes
for all to hear:
the politicians
and the high kings
hidden in their
lofty palaces,

the people gathered
at street corners
hoping to hear
sonatas of peace,
the poets and sages,
all wisdom drowned in
the wide sea of greed,
all compassion pressed
by the leaden brick
of human power.

TIME STRETCHES

Time stretches behind me
resurrecting memories
of now lost hours from shadows
that hide from the light.
Time stretches ahead as well, a
tunnel of time lit by hope
or darkened by muted fear.

I climb the ropes and ladders
connecting the minutes of
weeks, years and decades
as quickly and easily
as if I were still young
as if all time were unknown
as if its baskets were empty.

THE LITTLE SPARROW: A FABLE

Little sparrow, you still jump
onto the finger of my
imagination, poised with
the same poignant beauty
of six long lost decades
ago, when I held you

in my soft child's hands,
protecting you after
you had lost your mother,
soon after I had lost
my own. Eyes like berries,

soul so vibrant resting
in the nest of my palms,
I prayerfully held the
life entrusted, then perched
at the edge of his world.

Not yet ready to fly
but fully able to fear
he trembled before destiny,
the canons of fate booming,
soon to claim his so brief days.

Crushed by a young friend's misstep,
a cycle of time complete,
not without loss, not without grief,
the little sparrow was borne
to memory's vast, imperfect house.

WHEN YOU ADDRESS GOD

When you address God, make sure
your mind is open to suggestions
such as: building homes for displaced
animals, i.e. deer, raccoons and
owls in need of habitats NOT
for humanity. Or perhaps
you'll hear that the earth we share
has more than it needs of disease,
war, pollution and cruelty
and less than it needs of kindness,
healing, missions of peace and
general tidiness. Well, then,

perhaps you've heard all this before,
perhaps you've given it lip service.
You've assuredly listened with
a somewhat cynical ear to the
politicians multiplying like
cloned Pinocchios, noses stretched
around the sobbing equator,
blowing out their hot air wrapped in lies.
So, when you address God, make sure
your mind is open to suggestions.

IT'S A BEAUTIFUL DAY

It's a beautiful day
on the planet,
azure sky and dune grass
in agreement near the
mirrored bay, fall flowers
opening to receive due
accolades for their beauty,
shimmering iridescently
close to an almost empty
beach. No kite interrupts
an unblemished canopy,
no cloud travels a single
path toward the horizon
while I, seated at the table
of this visual feast,
inhale the September breeze
that rests near my waiting heart,
sacred memory stored within.

FLYING HIGH OVER HEDGES

Flying high over hedges, lost
in my inner child's dream,
I have no fear of falling.
I can hear my laughter
bouncing off the cars below.
I can smell the burning
of the autumn leaves, smoke
tickling the soles of my feet.
I can feel the infinite joy
of my immortal child
frozen in a memory that
grows more precious with time,
more perfect than the pale jewel
of tonight's smiling moon.

ANOTHER ANNIVERSARY

It's funny how anniversaries
can sneak up on you, appearing
at first in random subconscious
flashes or in an insomniac's
dream, so late in the night it's almost
morning. Then the shadows from your
mind look darker than midnight in
a moonless, starless, endless parade
of hours, hours that recall without rest
the memory you most need to forget.

I have such a memory and such
an anniversary, born on the
day my sister died twenty-five
years ago, carried away by the
demons of cancer, who hid in
the corners of her body until
she was consumed. Not surprised by
death, she was waiting for it with
courage, and left in its arms to
become part of the infinite dream.

How strange that at age sixty six I
still have a sister of thirty eight,
frozen in my dreams before she was
ill, vibrant eyes and copper hair
shining with intensity and strength,
awaiting with certainty the years
that should have paraded in order
past youth, maturity and old age,
past all the anniversaries that time
and life should have brought to her door.

SOME PAIN

Some pain never goes away
no matter what they tell you—
It arrives on that fateful
day with the sharpness of steel
razors to slice your naked heart
with lasting efficiency,
scar tissue binding more tightly
as years may pass while memory,
that magic genie of smoke
and illusion, sets up house
in your attic rooms, souvenirs
decorating endless high walls
with flashbacks, dreams and nightmares
until sleep becomes the enemy
of all sanity, swallowed in
a maelstrom of spiraling grief.

WHEN THE LONELY TIME COMES

In October, when the
lonely time comes to
Provincetown, I am ready,
body open to images
that rush at me, filling
my mind and heart with
metaphors and yearning.

That is when my arms ache,
heavy with poems that need to
fly free in their solitude.
That is when poetic
voices call my name,
rising from gold wired
cages hanging in my
multilayered soul.
Images cascade in a

waterfall of words.
A basket of metaphors
is delivered to a
double locked door that is
opened only by the key
of my pain. Music
I have heard in a dream
surges, music conceived in
heaven, written on earth.

THE PALE MOON RISES

The pale moon rises
over the lone dune shack,
solitary and poignant,
a cream colored fruit
ripe with promises and myths
that new lovers like
to recite in their bed,
floating around the room
beneath the pale moon rising.

OCTOBER BRINGS

October brings careening winds
levitating over surf in turmoil.

October brings an empty beach,
high blown clouds, a lonely path
for me to wander near the
churning bay, a perfect day
painted on a silver screen,
translucent over dune grass
and wild water, flowers
still blazing with early Fall
intensity in their pots
on my abandoned deck, my
eyes mesmerized by the far
horizon ablaze with light.

October brings me my pen
and waits for my response.

HANNAH'S EYES

Hannah's eyes,
beautiful baby
depths of wisdom
not yet aware
of the joys and
tragedies of
the spiraling
planet we know,

but reaching my
grandmother heart
with such ease,
with such poignancy,
they could be the
ancient eyes of love
that have always
visited my dreams.

IF LIFE BEGAN IN THE SEA

If life began in the sea
brine becoming blood,
pulsing with molecular
energy eons before
geography was known,

Why, then, must it be spilled
on ubiquitous battlefields
flooded with dying sighs
as mountains grieve the loss,
snow tears melting in anguish?

FLIGHT ON A BICYCLE PATH

The bicycle path twists
endlessly at the bottom
of the imposing dune
and I, breathing energy
deep into laboring
lungs, plunge even deeper
into the mystic forest as
birds screech a message to
their friends, "Bicycle Below,"
and squirrels disappear
to avoid confronting me.

The path elevates itself
then plunges downward
without warning, intrepid
and courageous, unafraid
of chance encounters. My
muscles tighten as the
sleek bike seems to defy
gravity, flying in
solitary silence, my
soul floating slightly above
my helmet. Then, heaven

suddenly appears at
the end of the trail as
the wild Atlantic roars
its welcome beyond the last
dune, now resting under a
sky so intensely blue
and deep, it swallows all
sense of time after the small
miracle of my flight.

IT'S A SWEET LIFE SOMEWHERE

It's a sweet life somewhere
peace holding hands with love,
eyes shining at children
learning the golden rule
from the ancient spirit
of light, but all I see,

at least for this moment
in time, at least on this
planet that we call earth,
whirling on its axis
of self created hate,

is a channel of greed
stuffing itself daily
with the food of power,
gold heaped in the banks of
destruction and pain,

while I search endlessly
that image from my dream,
that image now erased
on the blackboard of war,
as I repeat the lost refrain,
"It's a sweet life somewhere."

ON BECOMING A STAR

For I am made of the same
material that was once a
star, energy recycled.
But for this mini moment
in uncountable eons

I am in a conscious state,
contemplating and learning
creating and loving
looking at the stars above,
before the matter that is
I becomes perhaps a star

once more, hanging without
awareness in a firmament
of dreams and smoke that may
drift by your open window
some unknown and mystic day.

LAST WEEK I DREAMED

Last week I dreamed of Marjory Brown
returning to my classroom with
her textbooks that she said were no
longer of any use to her.
"Could you give them to someone?" she
wanted to know, a gray sadness
playing about her lovely eyes,
a tenuous smile disappearing
as she explained she was pre-law
and Spanish texts were not needed.
I took the books and thanked her for
her kindness to unknown others,
and said good-bye without thinking,
although I now feel something tugged
at my soul, a tug of warning.

When next I heard of Marjory Brown
it was from a newspaper that
announced her death, a suicide
from a bridge over the Delaware,
jumping from her own confusion
jumping from misunderstanding
jumping from the woman she loved
jumping from a family that could
not accept her as she had to be.
But it was only yesterday
after reading a poem to a
woman she would have resembled
had she lived, that I remembered
my grief, that I remembered her
plea and our unknowing farewell.

ELEGY FOR TWO FISHING BOATS

The Pat Sea and the Joan & Tom,
historic wooden fishing boats
in our small New England town, having
traveled Provincetown's deep harbor
for decades, sank to the bottom of
Cape Cod Bay without witnesses.

One sister ship sadly filled with
leaden black water, pulling her
mate to the depths while salt tears
collected at the bottom,
and ghostly images emerged
at low tide next to Macmillan
Pier. It was Sunday the ninth

of October when the twin deaths
occurred, history swallowed in
a rainstorm of loss, history
diminished in Provincetown but
immortalized in the paintings
of awed artists from everywhere.

AT THE DEPTHS OF MIDNIGHT

At the depths of midnight
my ship of sleep seeks a
safe harbor without dreams
as I sail into a fog
of memory and loss,
my inner screen painted
with the faces of the
now lost people from
my past, no longer more than
mist, as I steer the ship
toward daylight, toward hope
toward the soon east rising sun.

POEMS MAY EMERGE

Poems may emerge
from hiding places
in the dark night of the soul,
the recesses of memory
or a child's illumination.

Poems are retrieved
as they lie waiting,
images escaping freely
from crescendo borne waves
or the sad blaze of October.

Poems will travel
their bifurcated path
through the spirals of time,
past joy and redundant war,
to the very core of your heart.

I SAW A CHILD

I saw a child on the train
traveling north to San Juan
Capistrano, her smiling eyes
fixed on the Pacific, her
musical laughter bouncing
off the tired travelers
seated around her, piercing
the air with the open joy
of an unmarred heart and an
unblemished vision, soaking
up the California sun
and setting it free at once.

BEFORE YOU BECOME INMORTAL

Before you become immortal,
soul immersed in the white light
that conceals all earthly darkness,
open your slightly used eyes
to the beauty that evades you
to injustices around you,
seemingly invisible but
only superficially dressed
in the raiment of dismay.

Tear off the mask that now obscures
your heart, take out the coins of love
that, unused, still fill your pocket
with the leaden weight of the self,
and cast them quickly about you.

A PLACE TO PRAY

When I stand at the Wailing Wall
in Jerusalem, I pray that
my plea for peace will reach the ears
of the Lord. When I kneel at
Saint Peter in Chains, I am bound
to the gospel of love that Christ
whispered to the soul of the world.
When I complete my pilgrimage
to Mecca, I can hear a prayer
that carries me closer to paths
of wisdom lost to me before.

I can wear the symbols of all
the religions of the world close
to the palpitating beat of
my aspiring heart, but it is
at the profoundly azure sea
under the watchful canopy
of the mystic, all knowing sky
that I will hear my answer, that
I will offer up my grateful tears.

THE PEOPLE OF MY PAST

Sometimes I think I met
them in a dream, now lost
like smoke from a dead fire,
embers stored in boxes
that contain fear or pain,
anger or mystic love.

Sometimes the phantoms
fly past me at their will,
I unable to control
their pathways. They surge
from dormant or cyclical
memory, swarming like

monarch butterflies. They
light on my emotions
or inhabit my nightmares.
They are the people who
have crossed my bifurcated
path without warning

to become the photographs
that I select from time
to time, stored in my mental
wallet, now creased with age,
resting at the bottom
of a cluttered pocketbook.

THERE IS A POEM

There is a poem
waiting with patience
and untapped wisdom
that only you can
set free to wander.

It is both the child
and parent of your
message, still encrypted
in your memory
with golden emblems.

There is a poem
you will give to me
as I give mine to you
a token of our love,
birthright of our journey.

THESE ARE THE PEOPLE

Some people, colder than snow,
cover their hidden heart
with budding thorns, their
feet frozen in retraced
steps that lead to the core
of earth's ancient evils,
circling the globe without
rest. It would require
a monumental thaw
to melt down their pathway,

it would require sweet love
born in heaven's high hills
and transported by the
bright white light of Spring to
the lead heavy door of their
tundra house to release them
from their congealed glacier soul.
These are the people who
must sing with the winds of
war, who must nurture the plans

of their newest crusade,
written on the unholy
parchment of recycled death,
who appear on the news
with yesterday's story,
chanting the same promise
of ubiquitous terror
as it sears its path among
the blameless and those blamed,
blood roses painted on ice.

WHEN CHILDREN ARE STOLEN

When children are stolen,
singing on their way to
a fate they can neither
deter nor grasp until
it is upon them, seated
alongside the very
monster who deprives them
of their white innocence
and their very breath,

the loss is everyone's.
The pain and guilt belong
to those who thought but then
said nothing, those who feared
but forgot the moment, those
who watched but walked away,
as heaven welcomed the
song of the risen child
serenading at its gates.

PHOTO OP

It's time to film our stars,
Hannah and Jason
on the Provincetown Beach,
as their loud giggles wrap
around the tall dune grass
on a late November day
warmed by their mother's joy
under a cloudy then
bright blue Gemini sky.

It's time to make memories
while daring explorers
toddle across the sand
capturing a horseshoe
crab shell, stalking an
imaginary lion
in the dune dense jungle
or posing for Grandpa's old
movie camera held high.

It's time to send farewell
kisses across the sands of
time as Grandma and Grandpa
load up their southbound car
tomorrow, goodbye hugs
imprinted on inner
movie screens we will roll
out in sunny Florida,
technicolor flashing.

LOVE IN A WHITE BIRCH GROVE

Love in a white birch grove
is so simple, uncluttered by
unnecessary courtesies
or manmade structures of steel
and unbreakable glass.

There are only the silent trees
starkly arranged in small pale
groups, bark scarred by accidents
of birth or asymmetric
patterns crafted by passing storms.

There are only the ghosts of sighs
left behind by lovers, their
passion conceived on the moist green
moss where they once rested, after
the long lost war of their embraces.

THE ROAD OPEN TO ME

The road open to me
is the one I must follow
wherever it may lead
however it may challenge
the thoughts I now accept,
whoever may walk away
losing step with my own, I
sometimes stumbling often
running, now and again
lost in meditation,
pondering the inner path
that must be chosen
within my private world,
now bedecked in riches
and metaphoric beauty,
the road open to me.

A CHILD IN HER EIGHTIES

I saw her at the Golden Gate
Community Center, a child
in her eighties, thought arrested
in the mind of a three year old.

Her friend's bird had just died, she said,
tears streaming through the furrows of
her ancient face, fear and sadness
cloistered in soft, pale blue eyes that

she fixed on mine as I stood there.
"Can birds die?" she wanted to know.
"Will mine die?" she then asked of me.
"I don't think so, but if it does,

I know it will fly straight to Bird
Heaven, so don't you worry now."
She turned and scampered to her group,
happiness returned to young eyes.

PROPHECY FOR THE YEAR 3006

In the next millennium, now but a dream,
we will learn how to control spiraling time
horizontally and vertically,
moving from past to present effortlessly.
Memories will become relics of the mind,
permanent realities visited at will.

The potency of soaring intellect will
become more important than our physical
being, which will be slowly diminished,
our head housing an ever larger brain
capable of powers now unknown to us,
knowledge sought through emblematic processes.

Travel from dimension to dimension will
become a mundane experience for us,
but we will come to reject the concept of
heaven controlling our visible dimension
here on earth, assuming that it is we who
determine our convoluted destiny.

Discoveries will evolve from more complex
forms of intermittent communication,
some of which will become fused with our own
physical being, while other powers such
as telepathy and mind control will be
bestowed with advanced university degrees.

A mental and spiritual empathy
among all humans will be commonplace
as ancient mores and prejudice disappear.
And, although disease will no longer exist,
it will be replaced by a profound sense of

ennui at the loss of all risk and danger.

The focus of all adventure will be vast
intergalactic journeys. Soon new worlds
will form multiple states of the universe,
which may ultimately disintegrate if
man's irrevocable greed and need for
power emerge and dominate once again.

Children will seldom be produced, and therefore
will become the most prized and coveted
possessions of a human race whose physical potency
has dissipated, whose dreams of creation
are no longer realized on a whirling
planet that spirals toward infinity.

Then, man will certainly long for the simple
past, which those of the previous millennium
now inhabit, seeking to learn the secrets
of a time when we lived on an earth still green,
when love was expressed with passion and joy,
when man and his God were a personal dream.

FOLLOWING THE SUN----A VARIATION
To Jill and Matt

Following the sun, we
can almost see the path
to heaven straight before
our hearts, vows exchanged
in bright April under a
translucent white washed sky,
the soon setting sun semi
hiding in a twilight mist,
inviting us to watch
as it slides toward some
unknown infinity
in the unfolding story
of our sacred love.

There, our hands held
tightly inside a rose
colored channel, we
will seek the westernmost
seas that we can find,
our hands encircling the globe,
our open hearts embracing
the ancient path of love
to heaven, our radiant eyes
upon the now ascendant sun.

OIL CLOGS

Oil clogs the
arteries of
Washington,
sending it
into spasms
of greed that
work their way
out as far as
the Persian Gulf.

Oil clogs the
arteries of
Washington,
its once
vibrant heart
corrupted,
now stained
with Lincoln's
tears of grief.

Oil clogs the
arteries of
Washington,
polluting
the Potomac
with images
of tankards
now haunted by
phantoms of death.

I AM THE MESSENGER

I am the messenger
bearing grief and rage,
a pomegranate of
ruby passion painted
on the very top.

I am the messenger
bearing words of peace,
a midnight lightning storm
revealing the cherished Beth
across the stark white sky.

I am the messenger
bearing a cipher of love,
its burning letters
branding an errant message
onto my sighing soul.

LIFE OFFERS UP ITS POEMS

Life offers up its poems
unexpectedly, like roses
early in May or late in the
philosophic cycle that I
acknowledge daily.

They encapsulate my dreams,
delivered from surreal worlds
that I inhabit at night.
They raise my soul to the tops
of Spring blooming trees high

above the well traveled road below.
And from there I can breathe
the celestial air that escapes
from the unseen, unknown portals
leading me toward the gates of heaven.

SOMETIMES I THINK

Sometimes I think
I've spent too many days
contemplating what
death may be like.
Perhaps it is
a passage into an
unseen dimension that
exists side by side
with my present world.
Perhaps it is
a trip to nowhere
at all, the non perceived
black pit of anti-light,
a cocoon of nothingness.
Perhaps it is
a meandering stream drifting
into conscious thought,
images of prophets
displayed along the shore.
Perhaps it is
a three dimensional film,
Bogart and Monroe
at the ever moving bar,
toasting infinity.
Perhaps it is
a course contemplating
what life may be like,
an unusable return
ticket in my jeans pocket...
Sometimes I think
I'll spend eternity
contemplating what
life may be like.

58

I SEE THE IMAGE

I see the image...
It comes from sacred
memory, it haunts

me from the surreal
dreams I enter at
early morning hours.

I feel it surge from
earth and wind or a
heart heavy with grief.

I hold it in my
soul until it flies
from my pen, freeing

poetry paintings
to hang in galleries
along my joyous way.

AT THE FAIR IN PROVINCETOWN

They come to the fair in Provincetown
from everywhere in the wide world—
from Montreal and Paris, from Greece
and the Azores, from the Ukraine and
Australia, from the south of Africa
and the northernmost part of Finland.

They meet at the Unitarian
Church, on the small green lawn in front,
where artisans and a local poet
show their secrets of creation
to the locals and tourists alike.

Energy rises from tented booths
and the cacophony of voices as
multi languages merge in symphonies,
a symbiotic concordance of
art, understanding and the joy of
the swirling, celebrating brotherhood.

I NO LONGER GRIEVE

I no longer grieve for
the haunted child within,
now healed from all childhood abuse.

I watch her reach out to
other children lost in
the abyss of confusion
and pain that buries them,
that confiscates their joy.

I listen to her poems,
no longer written on
the wind, no longer penned
with the blood of disgrace
or the salted tears of grief.

I rejoice in the peace
that visits her daily, that
delights her sweet soul with its kiss.

IN THE DARKEST DREAM

Sometimes, in the darkest dream of
an interrupted and shallow sleep,
I come upon a clarity of
time and space as unexpected as
it is fleeting, and I thrust my soul,
naked and completely receptive,
into the precious moment that may
lead to revelation and joy. But,
before I can absorb the instant,
before I am able to inhale
its oxygen and celestial light,
it dissipates into the darkness
of the very dream that set it free,
disappearing before I can claim
what was my benevolent message.
Sometimes, in that darkest moment of
lonely loss and devastation,
I remember the clarity of
time and space, the yearning of my soul.

IN A SUMMER OF RAIN AND SHADOWS

In a summer of rain and shadows
darkening my solitary deck,
still subtly jeweled with the flowers of
ebbing July, I sit surrounded

by the wind from the bay and my thoughts
of summers now anchored in memory,
an indefinite longing ebbing
and waning as the Midsummer Moon,

with its orange and sinister eye,
begins to emerge from a pewter,
heavy lidded sky, lead colored clouds

soon covering the horizon then
obscuring the moon, my heart heavy
in a summer of rain and shadows.

IN THE POET'S WORLD

For in spite of its contradictions
its strange vagaries and cruelty,
despite its dependence on mere chance
and casual encounters that might
lead to monumental tragedies,

she came to love and cherish the world
in which she found herself. With its vast
seas to entice her from her study,
with its chameleon sky to test
her sense of color and clarity,

with its sacred woods to mystify her,
with its earth intended for her rest,
the poet walked out into the vast
beauty and ugliness that circled
her heart and mind, where she gave her thanks,

where she took root with her images
of love, hope and deep desperation,
a tree of poems bearing its fruit
among the lilies and thorn bushes
of a manic depressive universe.

THE HAWK SEEKS ITS PREY

The hawk seeks its prey
as I search the sea
for golden metaphors
and poems left behind
on ambivalent shore.

I gather them to my
hungry poet's heart,
then set them free once more
to wander through pages.
They seek a willing ear

accustomed to music,
to painting with poems
as the hawk flies above,
energy expelled
from darkly beating wings.

BUT ANGELS WHISPER

I.   But Angels Whisper

I must confront my pain
with open arms and truth,
my so familiar friend
that trails me as closely
as my shadow, leaving
lengths of light and darkness
along bifurcated roads.

But angels whisper prayers
of healing, poems of joy,
a subtle passacaglia,
and I must listen to
their Celestine whispers
as I follow my path,
as I sing my next song.

II.   Angels Whisper Poems

Angels whisper poems
into my hungry ear

poems stored in secret files
behind emerging clouds

shapes transfiguring
the sky with metaphors

emblems that fly to
my mind, my heart, my

ever racing pen,
whispers metamorphosed

into moments of joy,
sonatas of peace.

III.   Let the Angels Whisper

Let the angels whisper words
written in heaven, now lost
to the deaf ear of war, of death
so ubiquitous it squeezes
the planet in a leaden
vise of greed, devastation
and man devised pandemics.

Let the angels sing verses
conceived in heaven, let them
seize the loudspeaker of peace,
roaring over the battle
cries, branding our hearts with
messages of their love,
their golden calligraphy.

MAY YOUR PATH BE STREWN WITH POETRY

May your path be strewn with poetry
as it illuminates your dreams;
May verse fill your heart with images
as its wisdom guides your life.

May you journey with the sages
to a place not known before;
May they lighten all your burdens
as they open crystal doors.

May you gather golden metaphors
as love colors all your thoughts
as you travel on your pathway,
as your soul ascends toward sky.

THE WINDS CARRY MEMORY

The winds carry memory
to places visited before,
to friends who no longer
sojourn where I am wont
to be, to dreams that linger
like love lost long ago.

The winds carry heartache,
nostalgia and joy
first hidden, then revealed—
(What life was once made of
What life still is made of
What life still expects to be.)

MY PATH

My path must be inward,
convoluted it's true,
not one you may look for
but one that has found me

here where I am sitting
watching wind visit sea,
listening to the sound
of heartbreak near the dunes

that stretch indifferently
toward the fog misted arm
that holds the lighthouse close
to the root of the sand,

as my footprints evolve
from the beach to my heart
where my journey begins,

fireworks pulsing like
wild rain into limitless
sea and the now surprised sky

BLUEFISH FRENZY

The bluefish jump near Herring
Cove Beach, water twisted
into coils of hunger,
driving them toward a wild
voracious feast at the
shore's edge. I watch them as
they leap instinctively,
the dance of life and death
that will mark survival
under the indifferent,
gray bearded sky that
watches, but has no comment.

A SIMPLE PLACE

A simple place.
Uncluttered beach
some grass thatched dunes
a green-black sea.

A simple place.
Evocative
and sensuous,
yet filled with the

images of
struggle and life,
beauty and joy
water and sky.

All the things you
could wish for in
a simple place
--or anywhere.

SAND STEPPING AT LOW TIDE

Sand stepping at low tide,
through foot cooling pools and
cleansing seaweed, washes
last night's dreams of terror
from my wandering mind.
Schools of minnows, tiny
victims of diminishing
water, swim toward open
sea escaping the rising
sandbars, while hermit crabs
run from children's tiny
fingers and loss of freedom
in bright yellow buckets.

Nightmares evaporate
as the bay recedes from
the overheated beach.
They rise up to meet the
low flying clouds I think
I might be able to touch,
perhaps to hitch a ride
to the world where fantasy
abides, where images
reside, where visions are
controlled by my inner eye,
where high tide never comes
where horizon must meet me.

REVEALING MY WORLD

Revealing my world
of truth and mystery
with my racing pen

as wild images
fly like long lost birds
from the depths of my heart,

I open the book
of my painted poems
for all who wish to see—

The ink comes from my
salted, ancient tears,
the paper from trees

rooted in my secrets,
metaphors excavated
from the core of my soul.

WHEN I WAS

When I was young and motherless
I found nurturing in my books.
When I was pre-pubescent and
abused, I found good fathers in
the works of Homer, Shakespeare
and the Bible, models that would
take root in my marriage, my
dreams and my early poems.

When I was a teacher I sought
the children who were lost, in need
of faith, of truth, of kindnesses,
and there were many, so hungry
for a world of love and justice.
When I was a mother I held
my beloved children in the
deepest, most sacred corners of
my sometimes grieving heart, my tears
cleansing the lost child within me,
saving her pain and images
for the world I soon would reach.

But it was when poetry rushed
from me as I entered my sixth
decade, that wind and earth
released the metaphors of my
life, my pain, my joy, my world,
flying from my layered thoughts, my
open heart, my healed child within,
who now walked without pain,
almost floating in ascension.

75

BALLAD OF THE BROTHERS OF THE BOOK

Part One.

Their paths became separate
their dark destiny the same
when two half brothers parted
from one father, Abraham,
each destined as a patriarch
to Peoples of the Book, two
nations entwined in eons
of destruction led by
traditions that kept them apart:
Ishmael, the elder, born
to the handmaiden of Sarah,
expelled from his father's home
through no fault of his own. And
Isaac, a gift of the Lord,
then placed on a fiery altar,
almost sacrificed, and bathed
in Abraham's hot tears.
What dark thoughts would have traveled
with Ishmael, as he walked
to unknown lands alone? And
what thoughts would have pierced Isaac's
peace, his very core, more sharply
than the waiting knife? What thoughts
would sour his soul forever
as the Angel of Death waited?

Part Two.

Two half brothers soon parted,
each on his own path of faith
each on his own path of war,

76

fated for unending years
to spill the other's shared blood.
Half brothers of the Holy
Book, spilling poppy red blood,
mixed with the sand and water
of an oasis enshrined
in hate. Yes, two half brothers,
and when they were too tired
to count the hours of their days,
and when they were too old
to remember the birth of their scorn,
their children and their children's
children would remember as they
filled the Holy Land with their
rage and their wars and their graves.
Thus they walked the very path
that became bifurcated
but that is really the same,
and no one remembers that
two half brothers were begat
by Abraham, begat in love,
but lost in a desert of hate.

ON THE NIGHT OF THE APOGEE MOON

On the night of the apogee moon
(its face fullest its orbit widest)
magic descends from sky to my pen,

from deepest starry night to the town
I have come to love more than any
other, to the roads that wind through the

coyote visited dunes adrift
on this singular night of nights,
when the end of summer orb displays

its orange globe, low and resplendent,
further away but burningly close,
singeing the earth with its phantom beams,

its eternal patience painted on
infinite navy, its subtle light
pulling me as close as dreams allow.

On the night of the apogee moon
(its face fullest its orbit widest)
magic descends from sky to my pen.

WINTER WAITS

Joy stalks the low tide shore
while two small children scream,
piercing the translucent air
as they compete with flocks
of birds just thinking of
heading south. Late September
enters wearing vibrant tones,
her cooler breath displacing
the dune grass delicately.

Winter waits in the wings,
too polite to disrupt
this tranquil scene, precise
in its beauty, knowing
this late summer palette
will leave the party soon
enough, no need to crash, there's
time to fill his sand buckets
with his white and icy paint.

POEMS MAY FLY

Poems may fly from the grief of my heart,
from the wisdom of my soul or the depths
of earth's core. They may arise on a night
when the apogee moon teases the stars
with its mystery and its illusion.
Poems may fly from chance encounters, a
dream that enters reality with scorn,
or emotion that dissipates from waves
punishing shore intermittently. They
may fly beneath your wayward, weary feet
or over your exuberant head, but
rarely will they fly directly to you.
And so I ask of you, "Will you catch them?"

IF MY TIME IS SHORT ON THIS PLANET

If my time is short on this planet
(as measured by Indian counted
moons, or a Mayan calendar that,
encrypted in stone, declares twelve
twenty one twelve as the end of days),
then I must remember the advice
I know I have gleaned from my heart,
poignant words from my treasure of hours.

I must learn to fly with the condor,
higher into the mystical realm
of my own inner world, where my thoughts
propel me to the path of the moon
to the heart of the secret forest
to the soul of my own haunted child,
to the magic of my flying carpet.

I must learn to gather images
placed in time's solitary basket
which—at will—I can carry, set free
or plant in the ever fertile ground
that nourishes all that I will need
to slow the spiral of centuries,
to face the onslaught of eons,
verse ascending through my years of love.

BETWEEN EARTH AND SEA

Between earth and sea you
 will see me alone, as
 I watch dancing dune grass
finely stenciled in green,

growing graciously high
on sand roller coasters
that will move soundlessly
toward chameleon sea,

birds overhead flying
in disordered designs.
There are dream bearing clouds

that I think I can reach
as I sit here alone,
between earth and sea.

BETWEEN EARTH AND WIND

Between earth and wind
I can feel the moon's pulse
pulling tides and my heart
to a slow rhythmic beat.

I can see whirling dreams
rise above sea and surf,
pictures painted on mist
disappearing toward sky.

I can smell love's perfume
intertwined in your hair,
emanating from earth

as your feet touch the soil,
as your lips must meet mine
between earth and wind.

BETWEEN EARTH AND SKY

Between earth and sky
there are shadows and light,
there are images fading
or painted with tears.

There are secrets long gone
and circuitous paths,
there's both fable and truth
sung in ballads and chants.
There is pain, there is love,
there is heartache and war.

But beyond all these things
there is you, there is I,
and a journey that's destined
between earth and sky.

APHRODITE'S SONG OF SICILY

APHRODITE'S SONG

On a high lonely hill in Segesta
winds carry ancient messages
between Doric columns heavy as lead.
I can smell Aphrodite's fragrant breath
where her altar should have been, her poem
also written on the wind, its letters
drifting as far as unanchored dreams of
 love lost in time, its convoluted folds
wrapped around memory and earthly pain,
swirling about me as I face the views.

And I think that I can hear her whisper
her queries into my receptive ear:
"Who built this temple in my sacred name?"
"Whose hands forgot the altar that is mine?"
"Which name is yours that comes to sanctify
the ages lost now carried on the wind?"

FROM ANY MOUNTAIN IN SICILY

The fear of falling follows
my steps, unwelcome shadows,
shroud of misbegotten thought
that wraps itself around all
sense of weightless liberty.
The abyss below calls me,
its siren song bouncing off
ancient mountains, volcanoes
and cliffs suspended in
my wild imagination.

They lead me to their very
edge, tempting me to follow
phantom notes of mystery
to certain oblivion.
But like Ulysses I will
remain, tied with silken cords
to the mast of my courage,
where my stoic upturned eyes
can drink elixir from a
blue, phantasmagoric sky.

PALERMO: FIRE IN THE YEARS OF THE SPANISH INQUISITION

They came to watch
burning flesh that
had refused to
convert, to reject
Moorish or Jewish
heritage, lost
in roaring flames
that consumed all
that had been conserved
for centuries.

They came to watch
burning flesh as
to a circus,
entertained by
ashes rising,
high screams piercing
the smoky clouds
of vaporized
remains, cinders
heaped with remorse.

They came to watch
burning flesh as
conversion was
complete, although
they did not know,
as they smugly
watched the free show,
that they had lost
their own dark soul,
buried under ash.

IN THE CITY OF ONE HUNDRED CHURCHES

In the city of one hundred churches
there lived a so called man of honor, bound
by duty to "omerta," his family
controlled by the silence of "omerta,"
honor bound to maintain silence, but this
so called man of honor lost his control
when his brother-in-law, a traitorous
informant, broke the silence so imposed.
In the city of one hundred churches
called Corleone, heart of the lion,
silence was broken into small pieces,
scattered on the streets of Corleone,
and it came to pass that the Mafia
required a healing of blood and vengeance
from the man of honor whose compadre
had betrayed the pledge of holy silence.

In the city of one hundred churches
surrounded by cubist landscapes painted
by a hand more artful than Picasso's,
the man of honor was challenged with an
offer that he could not deny, in truth
an offer that would preserve his honor,
a choice to keep his own dear life intact,
a choice between his breath or another's.
And so this so called man of honor made
his dark decision, somewhere between the
fires of hell and nightmares best forgotten,
and on the day of the bells, in her home,
wedding dress on, hanging from a coarse rope,
was found his beautiful young wife, betrayed
by the still breathing man of honor, heart
darkened for eternity in his hell.

88

SOMETIMES A LITTLE POEM

Sometimes a little poem
will knock inside my head.
It stubbornly ignores
my efforts to repress it,
to convert its energy,
or to change its willful ways.
It will reverberate
inside me, perhaps keeping
me awake some quiet
moonstruck night, calling my name
until I open the door
to my soul. It rushes in,
colliding with mere menial
thoughts, rudely pushing them from
my conscious, mundane mind as
it leads me to my waiting
desk, where it will greet my pen
with a great sigh of relief.

THERE IS AN OLIVE TREE, THERE IS AN ALMOND TREE

In the Valley of the Temples
there is an olive tree, almost
deranged from twisting its bent arms
for slow moving long centuries
gathered near the lost catacombs
and the invisible altars
to the gods of I don't know when.

The olive tree chose not to be
the wood from which Jesus' cross
would be made, a cross requiring
wood that was straight, and ready to
be decorated with His blood.
The olive tree chose life not death,
its holy oil anointing the
most sacred moments of the Book,
from David to the Passover
from holiness to saintliness,
the soulful moments of our years.

But as I stood wrapped in my thoughts
the olive tree seemed to choose me,
its convoluted arms stretched out
to whisper at last its secrets,
while its onyx colored fruit spread
its carpet near my tired feet,
my open heart, my restless soul.

THERE IS AN ALMOND TREE, THERE IS AN OLIVE TREE

In the Valley of the Temples
there is an almond tree, beauty
fixed in place as by enchantment
for slow moving endless centuries
gathered near the lost plants called
mandrakes, screaming loudly near the
now poignantly empty altars.

The almond tree was once a girl
both delicate and beautiful
whose lover (she thought) had been killed
in the Trojan War and so chose
to leave her empty world behind.
But the gods pitied the loss of
such loveliness and created
the almond tree from her sweet soul.
The girl had chosen death, not life,
but she had been mistaken and
her lost lover returned safely.

And when her lover embraced her
the gods then blessed him with pity,
choosing love instead of dark death
and the almond tree acknowledged
his presence with showers of white
blossoms, laying a snow carpet
of love near his sorrowing heart.

IN THE VILLA OF CASALE

In the Vestibule of the Domina
the lady accompanies her children
to the baths, wearing elegant clothing.
She is Eutropia, wife and mother,
immortalized in hand placed tiles along
with two maidservants, their shadows behind
them, as I look down on a masterpiece
of flooring, bending over the railing.
There my own shadow creates another
near their rich robes, intersecting figures,
suspending an anachronism of
time and space. For now I seem to walk with
them, a ghost from the faraway future,
my thoughts above them bouncing off frescoes
that once were here, traces of yellow, red,
green and blue paint haunting my vision.

In the Owner's Bedroom the mosaic floor
is as complex as the emotions it
once contained, bouncing off polygonal
pillars that once supported erotic
thoughts of the Saturnalia, licentious
screams heard in the streets of Rome far away.
Dancing satyrs on pale blue background watch
the Owner and his concubines making
love in all the seasons, now frozen in
an eternity drunken with orgy,
passion and unending lust screamingly
braided in a mosaic of excess, as
I conjure a life of phenomenal
riches, now lost in the way of all dreams,
floating like mist into the endless years
lining the villa's empty corridors.

GREEK THEATER IN TAORMINA

In retrospective awe
I enter what once was holy,
a theater for pleasure,
prayer and contemplation
constructed by the Greeks, then
confiscated by the Romans
as a theater for blood games.

From peace and from worship
to death's entertainment
wearing tragedy's mask,
while Mount Aetna keeps watch
through pillars of stone,
in horror and silence,
no comment required.

WHICH WAR IS THIS?

Which war is this that
rains images near
my weary eyes, sad
faces begging peace
and seeking solace?
Which war is this that
makes death celebrate,
rejoicing in his dance?
Could it be in Spain
or Gaza, in New York
or even Africa?
Which war is this that
dominates the news
with terror, bombings,
betrayal and rape,
blood puddles on earth
where children should play?
Which world is this that
cannot understand,
that cannot get it right,
no matter the price
no matter the pain?
Did it evolve from
high Heaven or Hell,
from anger or anguish
from nightmares or phantoms?
Which war is this that
visits all my days,
that fills me with grief
as history repeats
its mantra of hate,
resounding once more
against a dead brick wall.

IN SIRACUSA, AT THE GREEK THEATER

At the Greek theater the priests
sit in places of veneration
while the masses gather on stone
seats ready for the tragic plays
of purification and the growth
of their needy souls, hearts open
to the words of their poets.
From sunrise to sunset they will
contemplate, observe, and pay their
tributes to the ancient gods, a
treasury of offerings and poems as
they face the actors piously.

At the Roman altar, no joy
is found as Zeus readies himself
to accept the blood of oxen—
(four hundred and fifty creatures),
overwhelming all sense of smell,
all sense of decency, flooding
from altars conceived in yearnings
as ancient as human instinct,
as ravishing as old passions
and the wild sport of the bullring,
while my mind flies from the altar
toward contemplation, toward peace.

ON MOUNT ETNA

As I climb Mount Etna, I return
to the history of thousands of
years ago, while a halo of smoke
rises from one of the craters on
the far side of the mountain, bright red
and gold magma flowing downward in
laborious twin streams, energy
that will be converted into rocks
of cold lava. Villages on the
slopes will cry out in fear and anguish.
Then the wind must wrap around me as
I approach the wild, ancient summit,
threatening to crush me in defiance
of my visit on the treacherous road
winding so endlessly skywards.

Later, lava's blaze ricochets against
profoundly black sky, from valley to
summit, from distant sea to ledges
that gently or precipitously
threaten to cast me down near the rocks
of the Cyclops, as if Hercules
himself would throw me, a lonely stone
first rolling then crashing into sea,
the deadly noise reverberating
from Mount Etna to the churning water,
then back to the fireworks of the molten
magma, exploding starbursts in a sky
approaching midnight, diminishing the
sedate half moon suspended near the crest,
envious sighs unnoticed by the mountain.